15 Easy-to-Rea

Nursery Rhyme
Mini-Book Plays

By Nancy I. Sanders

SCHOLASTIC
PROFESSIONAL BOOKS

New York • Toronto • London • Auckland • Sydney
Mexico City • New Delhi • Hong Kong • Buenos Aires

Dedication:

With love to Nancy Lojas: As kindergarten teacher for our sons, Dan and Ben, your loving dedication, tender care, and creative guidance influenced our family in a wonderful way. —*Nancy I. Sanders*

Cover design by Maria Lilja

Cover and interior artwork by Anne Kennedy

Interior design by Sydney Wright

ISBN: 0-439-35530-3

Copyright © 2003 by Nancy I. Sanders

Printed in the U.S.A.

Published by Scholastic Inc.

3 4 5 6 7 8 9 10   40   09 08 07 06 05 04 03

Contents

Plays

Introduction

Young children love rhymes—and nursery rhymes are a perennial favorite. The rich heritage of these classic rhymes helps shape a child's character and bring wonder and delight to his or her world. The 15 mini-book plays you'll find in this collection introduce children to nursery rhymes in a fun, fresh way that promotes emergent reading skills and reinforces curriculum concepts.

While reading these plays, your students will giggle with delight over monkeys hanging upside-down and playing "Rock-a-Bye, Baby." They'll cheer for Hickory, the mouse who runs up and down the clock—in a race car! They'll eagerly anticipate the opinionated Miss Muffet's next move as she plays the star role in a movie production. You can use these humorous plays and the easy-to-use extension activities to strengthen children's reading skills and to enhance their skills in math, language arts, science, and social studies.

Introduce these classic nursery rhymes by sharing your favorite book version with children. Then invite students to add their own fun and excitement by dressing in costumes or creating puppets to perform the plays. Or simply have individuals or small groups read the plays aloud.

Enjoy these creative plays with your students—and give them the gift of precious childhood memories!

—Nancy I. Sanders

How to Make the Mini-Book Plays

1. Copy the mini-book pages.

✱ To use a copier with a two-sided function, remove the reproducible pages from the book. Set the copier to the appropriate settings, then copy each mini-book play page.

✱ If your copier does not have a two-sided function, copy the cover and page 4 of the mini-book. Place that copy into the paper tray, then copy pages 2 and 3 so that page 2 backs the cover and page 3 backs page 4. (If the play has 8 pages, repeat this process with pages 6 and 7 and pages 5 and 8.)

Regardless of how you make the two-sided copies, you may need to experiment to be sure the pages are aligned properly.

cover   page 2

page 3

cover

2. Model for children how to assemble the books.

✱ For a 4-page mini-book play, simply fold the single page in half card-style, with the cover face-up.

✱ For an 8-page mini-book play, fold each of the pages in half card-style. Then sequence and stack the folded pages with the cover on top. Staple the pages together along the folded edges to create a book.

page 3   page 7   page 5

cover   page 5
                page 6

cover   complete book

Curriculum Connections

Baa, Baa, Math Time
Math

Wooly Math Facts

Give students practice in ba-a-asic math facts with this wooly center activity. Here's how:

✳ Label each of three paper lunch bags with a different sum to represent math facts your class is currently learning, such as 8, 9, and 10.

✳ Cut 15 wool shapes from white construction paper. Then divide the wool into three sets of five.

✳ For each set, write different math facts on the wool to correspond to the sum on one of the bags. Also write the sum on the back of each piece of wool for self-checking purposes.

✳ Put the wool in a resealable plastic bag. Then place the wool and the lunch bags in your math center. (You might want to create additional sets with different math facts to add to your center.)

✳ During center time—or at any time students have a few extra minutes— invite children to practice their math facts with the bags and wool. To do so, they place each piece of wool into the bag corresponding to its sum. Children can check their work by simply peeking at the back of each piece to make sure it matches the number on the bag.

The Story of Hey
Diddle, Diddle
Language Arts

Books in the News

Promote reading skills by featuring students' book reviews in the pages of a newspaper.

Invite children to illustrate and summarize their favorite books. Make sure each child's work includes the book's title and author, as well as his or her own name. Then have children glue their "reviews" onto the pages of a recycled newspaper. Add the newspaper to your class library, then invite children to browse through the paper to read the latest literary reviews.

Race Around the Clock
With Hickory Dickory Dock
Language Arts

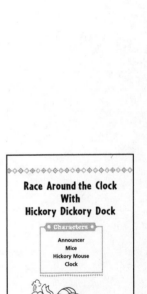

Adventure Sequences

Students' creativity will be off and running when they use this sequencing activity to make up their own adventure stories.

Give children half-sheets of 12- by 18-inch construction paper, cut lengthwise. Then ask them to find and cut out adventure scenes from magazines to glue in the center of their paper. Instruct students to draw scenes to the left and right sides of the picture to illustrate imaginary events that might have happened before and after the scene in the actual picture. Help children write captions under the pictures. Then invite them to share their sequenced adventures with the class.

Bill and his friend went on a trip to Africa.

They drove through the jungle in a jeep.

They saw dinosaurs!

The Humpty Dumpty Contest

Characters
Humpty Dumpty	King's Horses
Announcer 1	King's Men
Announcer 2	Child

The Humpty Dumpty Contest   Language Arts

Word Family Sort

Here's an "egg-cellent" way to reinforce word family sight words:

* Cut out 24 actual-size egg shapes from white construction paper. Divide the eggs into two sets of twelve.

* Label one set of eggs with words from a designated word family—such as *at, bat, cat, fat, flat, hat, mat, gnat, pat, rat, sat,* and *vat.* Then label the other set with words from a different word family. (For word families with fewer examples, you might use only six or eight eggs per set.) Mix all the eggs together in a basket.

* Label two egg cartons, one for each word family. Place the basket of eggs and cartons in a center.

* Invite pairs of students to place each egg into the carton that corresponds to its word family.

* Every few weeks, replace the eggs and cartons with new ones to represent different word families.

Little Boy Blue
Has a Job to Do

Characters
Cows	Villager 2
Sheep	Little Boy Blue
Villager 1	

Little Boy Blue Has a Job to Do   Social Studies

Our Community Helpers

Just as Little Boy Blue had a job to do, so do our community helpers!

As a group, brainstorm a list of community helpers. Then invite one child at a time to pantomime the role of a community helper from the list while the class sings:

"This is the way I do my job, do my job, do my job.
This is the way I do my job, in our neighborhood."

Challenge children to guess the identity of the community helper. Afterward, discuss the details of the worker's job.

The Case of the Missing Jack Horner   Math ✳

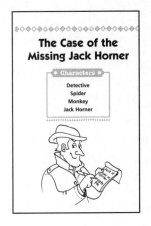

How Many Plums?

Children will find that addition and subtraction are as easy as pie with this fun activity.

Prepare one pie for each of four or five small groups. To make a pie, decorate the bottom of a paper plate to resemble the top crust of a pie. Cut a wedge from the pie top, then staple it to another paper plate to create a whole pie, as shown. Put 10 or more purple paper plums into the pie (or an amount appropriate to the skill level you are teaching). Then have groups solve word problems, such as the following, using their pies and plums:

✳ Jack took out four plums and then six more. How many plums did he take out altogether?

✳ A baker put three plums into an empty pie. Another baker added three more plums. How many plums are in the pie?

✳ There were 10 plums in the pie. Jack took out seven plums. How many plums are left?

Miss Muffet, the Movie Star   Language Arts ✳

It's Show Time!

Spotlight students' imaginations with these big-screen writing prompts.

Put pictures and/or a few small objects, such as a key, necklace, coin, or finger puppet, into several lidded plastic video boxes. Invite children to peek inside the box of their choice. Then have them illustrate and write an imaginary movie scene that uses all the objects in the box. Afterward, hold a special show time for children to share their movies (don't forget the popcorn!). These shows are sure to get rave reviews!

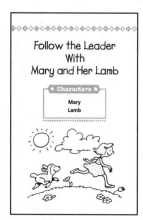

Follow the Leader With Mary and Her Lamb

Reasoning ✳

Find the Leader

Give students a reasoning-skills workout with this twist on Follow the Leader. To play:

✳ Seat children in a large circle on the floor. Ask one child to leave the room.

✳ Choose a volunteer to be It, the leader. Explain that It will begin an action that can be performed in place, such as clapping, nodding, or patting a foot. The rest of the children will imitate the action. Periodically, It will change the action, with the class following his or her lead.

✳ Have It begin an action. While the action is in progress, invite the child back into the room to stand in the center of the circle.

✳ As the class performs the different actions, the child tries to guess who It is. (So that children don't give away It's identity, encourage them to watch out of the corner of their eyes instead of looking directly at It.)

✳ After the child correctly guesses It, have him or her join the circle. Then send It out of the room to become the next guesser.

Pussy Cat, Pussy Cat, What Should We Do?

Dramatic Play ✳

Let's Solve the Problem!

Just as the guards solved Mouse's problem, students can come up with their own solutions to these true-to-life problems.

First, label notecards with problem situations that children can relate to—such as losing a cherished toy, being asked to eat a disliked food, and feeling left out of a friendship. Then ask pairs of children to pick a card, privately talk out a solution to the problem, and then act out their solution. Can the class guess the problem and the solution? Perhaps another pair can act out an alternative solution to the same problem.

Mother Hubbard's Empty Cupboard   Math

Math With Mother Hubbard

To help children bone up on their math skills, invite student pairs to take the roles of Mother Hubbard and her dog. Then have the pairs use a supply of the bone patterns (below) for the following activities:

* Ask Mother Hubbard to count up to 10 bones into a bowl for the dog (or a larger amount, according to students' skill level). Then have the dog return the bones—one at a time—to Mother Hubbard, counting backward as he or she removes them from the bowl.

* Label a supply of bones with numerals, then place them into a plastic cup. Ask Mother Hubbard and the dog to each pick a bone. Who has the larger (or smaller) number? Have them continue until all the bones have been removed. Then challenge the pair to arrange the bones in numerical sequence.

* Divide the bones into two equal sets. Stamp one of several different designs onto each bone in a set, creating two identical sets of bones. (Or use sticker designs, such as stars and hearts.) To use, Mother Hubbard creates a pattern of up to five bones with one set. The dog copies the pattern with bones from the other set.

* Combine the two sets of bones from above. Then have Mother Hubbard and the dog work together to sort the bones by symbols.

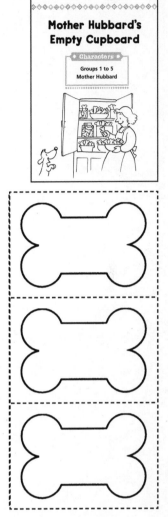

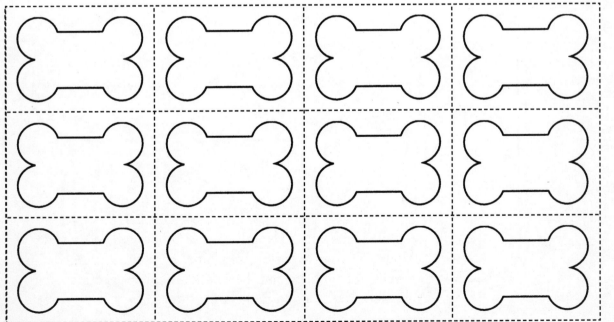

Happy Birthday Pat-a-Cake

Language Arts

Birthday Time at the Alphabet Zoo

"Cake-and-candles" day at the zoo is the perfect time to provide children with practice in matching upper- and lowercase letters. Here's how to prepare a learning center for this important skill:

✳ Cut out 26 copies of the cupcake and candle patterns below. Label each cupcake with an uppercase letter and each candle with a corresponding lowercase letter. Put the cupcakes on a plate and the candles in a cup.

✳ Cut out animal pictures from magazines or coloring books to represent each letter of the alphabet. Mount them on construction paper squares. For self-checking purposes, label the back of each animal with its beginning letter. Put the pictures in a basket.

✳ Place the cupcakes, candles, and animal pictures in a center.

✳ When students visit the center, invite them to choose an animal from the basket. Then have them "make" the animal a birthday cupcake by matching the cupcake and candle that corresponds to the beginning letter of the animal's name.

✳ As an extra challenge, encourage students to arrange the animals and cupcakes in alphabetical order. When finished, invite them to sing happy birthday to the entire alphabet of zoo animals!

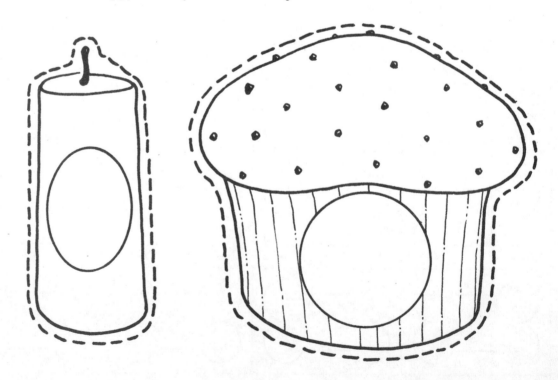

Rock-a-Bye, Baby, Swing on the Treetop Science

Animal Homes Collaborative Books

Many monkeys live in trees, but where do other animals live?

As a group, make a list of different animals and their homes (for example, fish/pond, bear/den, bird/nest, bee/hive, ant/hill, lion/cave, squirrel/tree, beaver/lodge). Then have students pick an animal and its home to draw on a sheet of construction paper. As an extra challenge, children might research their animals and write a few facts on their pages. Sort the student pages according to where the animals live—in the water, underground, in a tree, and so on. Then bind them into a class book.

This Little Pig Plays a Game Social Studies

Activity Journals

These activity journals can help your students discover how fun life can be without TV!

For each child, staple together a booklet of 10 half-sheets of paper. Then guide children in labeling each page with a different day and date for two weeks of school days. Send the booklets home with notes explaining that children should list each of their non-TV activities on the appropriate days. At the end of the two weeks, share and discuss all the interesting activities that children have listed in their booklets. To extend, children can graph their activities by type, such as "Games," "Cooking," "Reading," and "Sports," to find out which type of activity they participated in most.

Three Little Kittens Learn to Share   Reasoning

Whose Pie?

Add some creative flair to this pie-making activity and you'll have the perfect recipe for logical reasoning fun!

First send students to private areas of the room to draw decorated pies on paper plates. Ask them to adorn their pies with colorful stripes, circles, swirls, zigzags, and other interesting designs. Then, when you call the class together for this activity, ask children to turn their pies facedown so that other students cannot see them. Give each of three volunteers an index card labeled "Kitten 1," "Kitten 2," or "Kitten 3." Take the three kittens' pies, mix them up, and display them in front of the class. Explain that the three kittens will give clues to help the class guess which pie belongs to which kitten. Then have each kitten describe several features of his or her pie, such as designs or colors. After all the kittens finish their descriptions, invite students to cooperatively match each kitten's card to its pie. Did the class correctly guess whose pie is whose? Repeat the game until every student has a turn to be a kitten.

Wee Willie Winkie's Mixed-up Day   Math

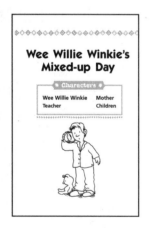

What Time Is It?

Tick, tock. Tick, tock. Time to set the giant clock. And this special clock uses real hands!

Draw a large "hand-less" clock—with a diameter of about three feet—on butcher paper. Mount the clock on a wall so that its center is about shoulder high to students. Then ask a volunteer to stand in front of the clock under the "12," as shown. Invite another child to be the timekeeper. As the class reads the play aloud, have the timekeeper position the volunteer's arms/hands to indicate each time that is mentioned in the play. After several rounds, add interest by inviting children to substitute different times into the play.

Baa, Baa, Math Time

Mr. Black Sheep: Very good!
Now I have 2 bags of wool.
I give 1 to my dame.
How many bags of wool
do I have left?

4

**Mr. Black
Sheep:** Good morning, class.

**Student
Sheep:** Good morning,
Mr. Black Sheep.

**Mr. Black
Sheep:** It's math time!
I have 3 bags of wool.
I give 1 to my master.
How many bags of wool
do I have left?

2

**Student
Sheep:** We add and subtract.
Math is lots of fun!
We count and work
the numbers out.
Soon the problem's done.
The answer is 2!

3

Student Sheep:

We add and subtract.
Math is lots of fun!
We count and work
the numbers out.
Soon the problem's done.
The answer is 0!

Mr. Black Sheep:

That's right!
Now I have 1 bag of wool.
I give it to the little boy
who lives down the lane.
How many bags of wool
do I have left?

**Mr. Black
Sheep:** Perfect!

Now it's nap time.

**Student
Sheep:** Great.

Let's practice counting people!

The End

**Student
Sheep:** We add and subtract.

Math is lots of fun!

We count and work

the numbers out.

Soon the problem's done.

The answer is 1!

$$2 - 1 = 1$$

The Story of Hey Diddle, Diddle

Characters

Child 1
Child 2

Child 1: It had a surprise ending!
The dish ran away
with the spoon.

Child 2: Oh! I love stories
with surprise endings!

Child 1: Why don't you read it, too?

Child 2: I will! I'll read it today!

The End

4

Child 1: I read a good story today!
It's called "Hey Diddle, Diddle"
by Mother Goose.

Child 2: Why did you like it?

Child 1: It had animals!
The cat played a fiddle.

Child 2: Oh! I love stories with animals!

Child 1: It had adventure!
The cow jumped
over the moon.

Child 2: Oh! I love stories
with adventure!

Child 1: It was funny!
The little dog laughed.

Child 2: Oh! I love stories
that are funny!

Race Around the Clock
With
Hickory Dickory Dock

Announcer: It's time for the race
to start!
On your mark.
Get set. Go!

4

Announcer: Here we are at the
Mouse Town Car Races!

Mice: Go, Hickory!

2

Announcer: Yes, the famous
race car driver,
Hickory Dickory Dock,
is getting ready
for her race
up and down the clock.

Mice: Go, Hickory!

3

Mice: Go, Hickory!

Hickory: Zoom! Zoom! Zoom!

Announcer: She's coming
down the clock!
She's crossed
the finish line!
She's the fastest mouse
in history!

Hickory: Zoom! Zoom! Zoom!

Clock: BONG!

Announcer: Did you hear that?
The clock struck one!
It's a new world record!

Mice: Three cheers for Hickory!

Announcer: Boys and girls all over
the world will talk about
this race for years to come!

The End

8

Hickory: Zoom! Zoom! Zoom!

Announcer: She's off!

Hickory: Zoom! Zoom! Zoom!

Announcer: There she goes
up the clock!
Look at that speed!

5

The Humpty Dumpty Contest

✸ Characters ✸

Humpty Dumpty	King's Horses
Announcer 1	King's Men
Announcer 2	Child

King's Horses: Neigh! Neigh! Neigh!
We will find a way.

King's Men: Let the contest begin!
We will be
the ones to win!

Announcer 1: Hear ye! Hear ye!

Announcer 2: The king's horses and
king's men will try first.

4

Humpty Dumpty: Here I am sitting
up on this wall.
Tip, top, tip.
Oh no! I'm going
to have a great fall!
CRACK!

Announcer 1: Hear ye! Hear ye!
The king is
having a contest.

Announcer 2: Whoever puts
Humpty Dumpty
together again
wins a chest of gold!

Child: I'll put these pieces here.
I'll put those pieces there.

7

Child: May I have a turn, please?

Announcer 1: Okay. The contest is open to all.

Announcer 2: Even little kids.

Child: There! I did it!

Announcer 1: You win!

Announcer 2: But you're just a little kid!

Child: Yes! Little kids can do big things!

The End

King's Horses: One piece, two pieces, three pieces, four.

King's Men: Putting this egg together is a very hard chore!

5

Little Boy Blue Has a Job to Do

**Cows and
Sheep:**   Look over there! Hay!

Cows: Munch. Munch. Munch.
We like to chew on hay
for lunch.

4

Cows: Moo! Moo! Moo!
This corn is good to eat.

Sheep: Baa! Baa! Baa!
The meadow grass
tastes sweet.

2

Villager 1: Hurry! Hurry! Hurry!
Go find Little Boy Blue.

Villager 2: The cows and sheep
are out of the barn.
Little Boy Blue has
a job to do.

3

Little Boy
Blue: Toot! Toot! Toot!

It's time for you to scoot!

Hurry! Run along!

Go back where you belong.

Cows and
Sheep: Uh-oh.

Look who's under
the haystack!

Cows: It's Little Boy Blue!

Sheep: Now what should we do?

Sheep: Crunch. Crunch. Crunch.
We like to eat a bunch.

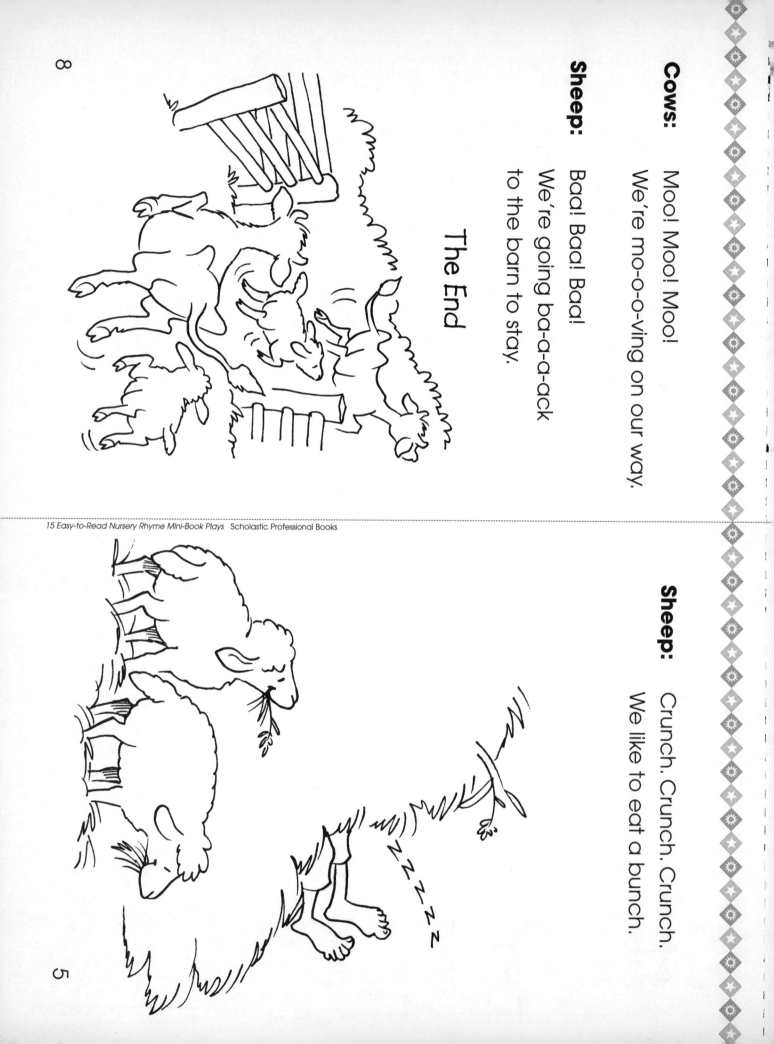

15 Easy-to-Read Nursery Rhyme Mini-Book Plays   Scholastic Professional Books

Cows: Moo! Moo! Moo!
We're mo-o-ving on our way.

Sheep: Baa! Baa! Baa!
We're going ba-a-ack
to the barn to stay.

The End

The Case of the Missing Jack Horner

Detective
Spider
Monkey
Jack Horner

Jack: I'm the REAL Jack Horner.

Detective: How can I know for sure?

Jack: I was sitting in a corner
eating my Christmas pie.
I put in my thumb
and pulled out a plum.

Detective: The case is solved.
You're the REAL Jack Horner!

The End

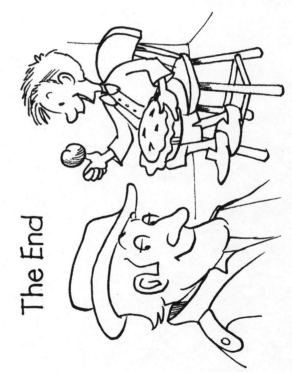

4

Detective: I'm looking for
the REAL Jack Horner.

Spider: I'm the REAL Jack Horner.

Detective: How can I know for sure?

Spider: I was sitting in a corner
eating the bugs in my web.

Detective: Thank you. I have all the clues
I need from you. Next?

2

Monkey: I'm the REAL Jack Horner.

Detective: How can I know for sure?

Monkey: I was sitting in a corner
eating a bunch of bananas.

Detective: Thank you.
I have all the clues
I need from you. Next?

3

Miss Muffet, the Movie Star

✳ Characters ✳

Little Miss Muffet
Director
Chorus

15 Easy-to-Read Nursery Rhyme Mini-Book Plays Scholastic Professional Books

Miss Muffet: It's made with milk.
It's good! Yum! Yum!

Director: That sounds silly, but okay.
Lights! Camera! Action!

4

Director: Lights! Camera! Action!

Chorus:
Little Miss Muffet
sat on a tuffet
eating a piece of pizza.

Miss Muffet: CUT!

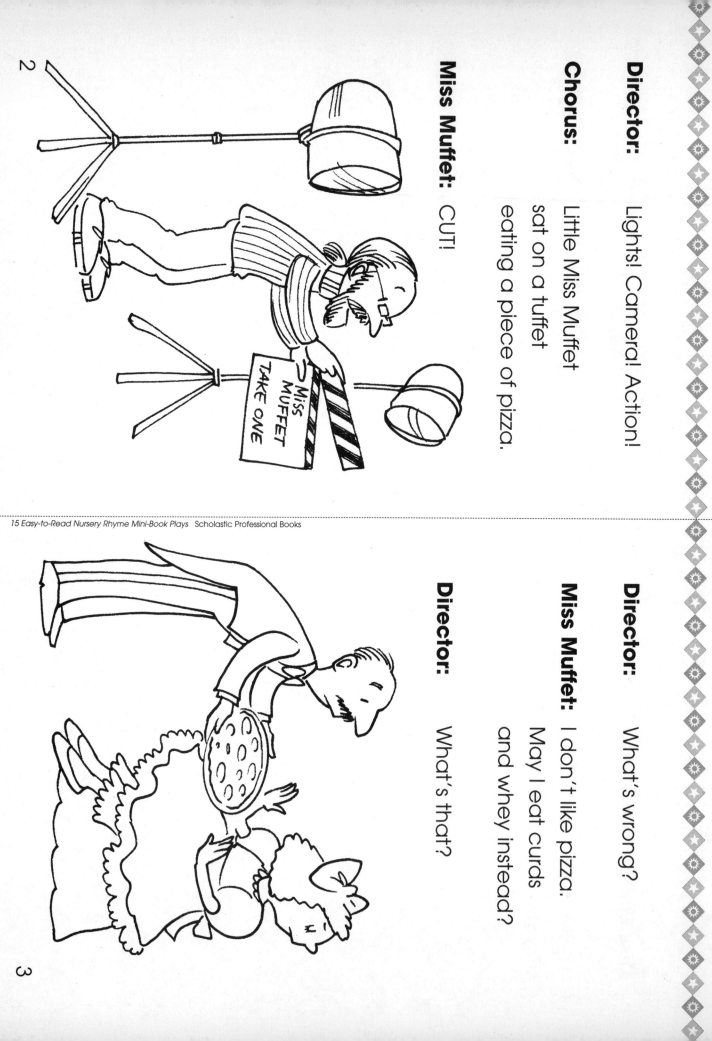

15 Easy-to-Read Nursery Rhyme Mini-Book Plays Scholastic Professional Books

Director: What's wrong?

Miss Muffet: I don't like pizza.
May I eat curds
and whey instead?

Director: What's that?

Director: Okay.
Let's use a spider instead.

Miss Muffet: But I'm scared of spiders.

Director: Great!
This can be a scary movie!

Miss Muffet: That sounds silly, but okay.

Director: Lights! Camera! Action!

15 Easy-to-Read Nursery Rhyme Mini-Book Plays Scholastic Professional Books

Director: What's wrong now?

Miss Muffet: Cats make me sneeze.
A-choo! A-choo!

A-CHOO

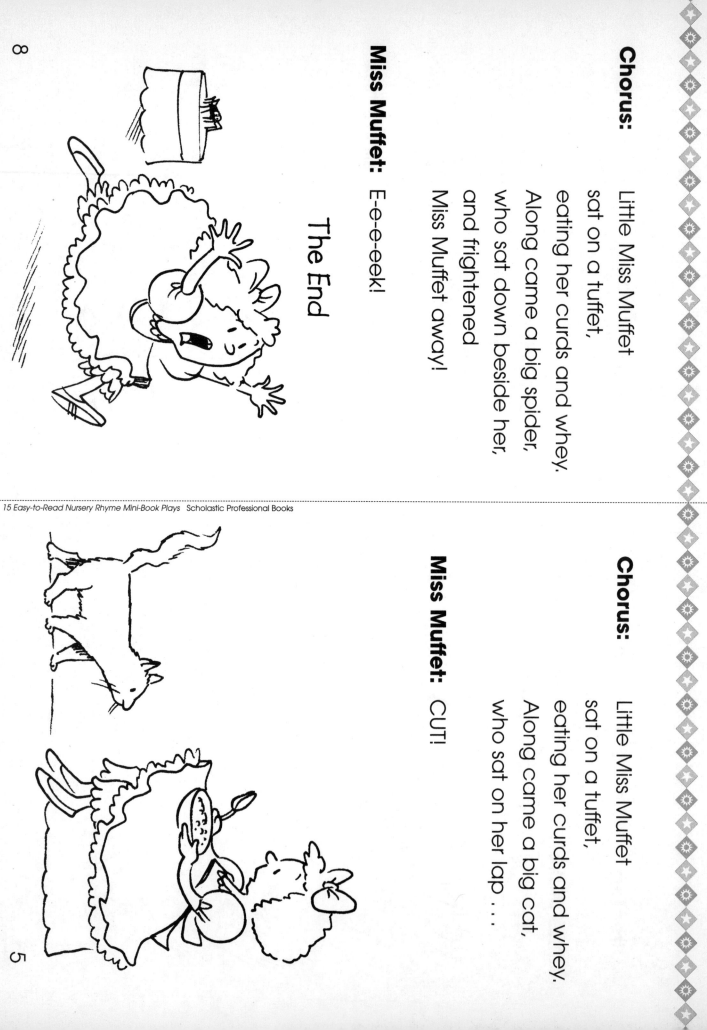

Chorus:

Little Miss Muffet
sat on a tuffet,
eating her curds and whey.
Along came a big spider,
who sat down beside her,
and frightened
Miss Muffet away!

Miss Muffet: E-e-e-eek!

The End

8

Chorus:

Little Miss Muffet
sat on a tuffet,
eating her curds and whey.
Along came a big cat,
who sat on her lap . . .

Miss Muffet: CUT!

5

Follow the Leader With
Mary and Her Lamb

Characters

Mary
Lamb

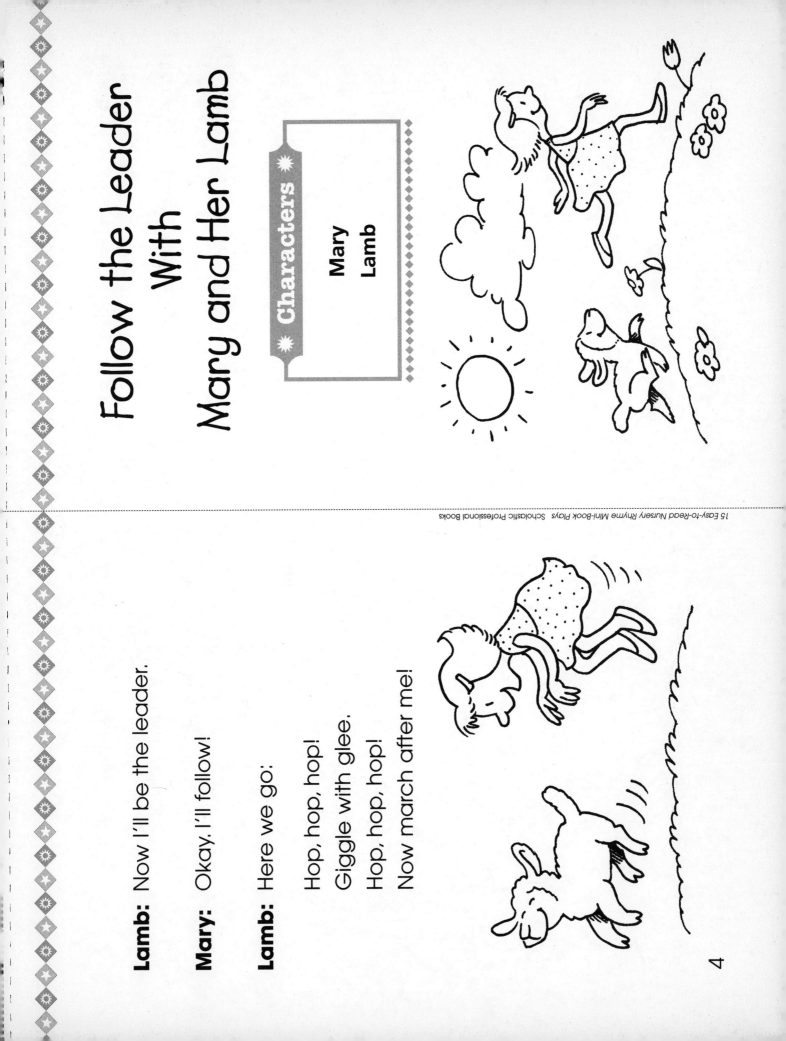

Lamb: Now I'll be the leader.

Mary: Okay. I'll follow!

Lamb: Here we go:

Hop, hop, hop!
Giggle with glee.
Hop, hop, hop!
Now march after me!

4

Lamb: Let's play Follow the Leader!

Mary: That sounds like fun!

Lamb: You be the leader. I'll follow!

Mary: Okay. Here we go:

Clap, clap, clap!
Pat your knee.
Clap, clap, clap!
Now skip after me!

2

3

Mary: Here we are at school!

Lamb: I followed you all the way!

Mary: We clapped and skipped.
And patted our knees.

Lamb: We hopped and marched.
And giggled with glee!

Mary: We jumped and jogged.
And buzzed like a bee.

Mary: Okay. Here we go:

Jump, jump, jump!
Buzz like a bee.
Jump, jump, jump!
Now jog after me!

Lamb: We had lots of fun,
Don't you agree?

Mary: Now it's time to
learn to read and write.

Lamb: May I learn, too?

Mary: Sure! Just follow along with
everything the teacher says.
You'll do great!!

The End

15 Easy-to-Read Nursery Rhyme Mini-Book Plays   Scholastic Professional Books

Mary: It's time to go to school.

Lamb: I'll come too!

Mary: That sounds like fun!

Lamb: You be the leader. I'll follow!

5

Pussy Cat, Pussy Cat, What Should We Do?

Characters

Queen	Guard 2
Mouse	Cat
Guard 1	

Queen: Guards! Stop those hiccups now.

Guard 1: Oh my! What should we do?

Guard 2: Look! It's a cat!

Cat: BOO!

Mouse: Squeak! Squeak! Squeak!
That cat scared me.
Now my hiccups are all gone!

The End

4

Queen: There's a mouse under my chair. It has the hiccups.

Mouse: Hiccup! Hiccup! HICCUP!

Queen: Guards! Stop those hiccups now!

Guard 1: Oh my! What should we do?

Guard 2: I know! Here, Little Mouse. Drink a cup of water.

Mouse: Okay. Hiccup! Hiccup! HICCUP!

15 Easy-to-Read Nursery Rhyme Mini-Book Plays   Scholastic Professional Books

Queen: Guards! Stop those hiccups now!

Guard 1: Oh my! What should we do?

Guard 2: I know! Here, Little Mouse. Stand on your head.

Mouse: Okay. Hiccup! Hiccup! HICCUP!

Mother Hubbard's Empty Cupboard

❋ Characters ❋

Groups 1 to 5
Mother Hubbard

Group 5: 1 little dog bone
sitting in the bowl.
Fifi ate 1 and then
she was full!

**Mother
Hubbard:** Oh my, little Fifi!
Look what you've done.
You ate all the dog bones
and now there are none!

The End

4

Group 1: 5 little dog bones
sitting on the floor.
Fifi ate 1 and then
there were 4.

Group 2: 4 little dog bones
sitting near a tree.
Fifi ate 1 and then
there were 3.

Group 3: 3 little dog bones
sitting in a shoe.
Fifi ate 1 and then
there were 2.

Group 4: 2 little dog bones
sitting in the sun.
Fifi ate 1 and then
there was 1.

2

3

Happy Birthday Pat-a-Cake

Characters

Zookeepers 1 to 3
Bakers

Zookeeper 2: Hurry! Hurry! Hurry!
A happy day is here!
The bear just had a baby.
Spring is finally here!

bear

4

Zookeeper 1: Hurry! Hurry! Hurry!
A happy day is here!
The ape just had a baby.
Spring is finally here!

2

Bakers: We'll bake
a happy birthday cake.
It's just the perfect size.
We'll put an "a" for ape on top.
Won't everyone be surprised!

3

Bakers: We'll bake
a happy birthday cake.
It's just the perfect size.
We'll put a "c" for camel on top.
Won't everyone be surprised!

15 Easy-to-Read Nursery Rhyme Mini-Book Plays   Scholastic Professional Books

Zookeeper 3: Hurry! Hurry! Hurry!
A happy day is here!
The camel just had a baby.
Spring is finally here!

All:

It's springtime at the zoo again.
We're having so much fun!
A special time! A happy time!
Whose baby is next to come?

The End

15 Easy-to-Read Nursery Rhyme Mini-Book Plays   Scholastic Professional Books

Bakers: We'll bake
a happy birthday cake.
It's just the perfect size.
We'll put a "b" for bear on top.
Won't everyone be surprised!

Rock-a-Bye, Baby, Swing on the Treetop

Characters

Monkeys 1 to 3

Monkey 3: YAWN! I'm sleepy!

Monkey 1: Let us rock you to sleep.

Monkey 2: Rock-a-bye, baby, on the treetop.

Monkey 1: We'll rock you and swing you.

Monkey 3: Whee-e-e-e! Please don't stop!

4

Monkey 1: Let's play house!
I'll be the mommy.

Monkey 2: I'll be the grandpa.

Monkey 3: I'll be the baby.
Waa-a-a!

Monkey 2: I made banana soup
for supper.

Monkey 3: I'm hungry, too!
Waa-a-a!

Monkey 1: Here's a bottle of
banana juice for you!

3

Monkey 1: Look at me!
I'm hanging by my tail!

Monkey 2: Look at me!
I'm hanging by my toes!

Monkey 3: Look at me!
I'm hanging by my arms!

15 Easy-to-Read Nursery Rhyme Mini-Book Plays   Scholastic Professional Books

All: Great! Here we go.

Monkey 1: Rock-a-bye, baby,
under the sun.

Monkey 2: We're rocking and swinging.

Monkey 3: Whee-e-e-e! This is fun!

All:

Let's play house again!

Rock-a-bye baby, on the treetop

We're rocking and swinging

Let's never stop!

Whee-e-e-e!

The End

Monkey 1: Now I want to be the baby.

Monkey 2: No. It's my turn!

Monkey 3: Let's all be babies.

All: Waa-a-a!

This Little Pig Plays a Game

15 Easy-to-Read Nursery Rhyme Mini-Book Plays   Scholastic Professional Books

✹ Characters ✹

Mama Pig	Little Pig
Sister Pig	Baby Pig
Brother Pig	Chorus

Little Pig: I'm bored!

Baby Pig: Me, too!

Little Pig: Let's watch TV.

Baby Pig: No. Let's turn the TV off.

Mama Pig: Let's play a game instead.

4

Mama Pig: Sister Pig is going
to the market.
Who wants to go along?

Little Pig: Not me! I'll stay home.

Mama Pig: Brother Pig is going out
to eat roast beef.
Who wants to go along?

Baby Pig: Not me! I'll stay home.

Little Pig and
Baby Pig: Come play a game with us!

Sister Pig and
Brother Pig: Okay! Hurray!

15 Easy-to-Read Nursery Rhyme Mini-Book Plays Scholastic Professional Books

Sister Pig: I'm back from the market!

Brother Pig: I'm back, too!

Sister Pig: Let's watch TV.

Brother Pig: No. Let's turn the TV off.

Chorus: Move the markers
round and round the board.
Turn off the TV. Play a game!
Then you won't be bored.

The End

**Little Pig
and
Baby Pig:** Okay! Hurray!

Chorus: Move the markers
round and round the board.
Turn off the TV. Play a game!
Then you won't be bored.

Three Little Kittens Learn to Share

Characters

Kittens 1 to 3
Puppies 1 to 3

Kitten 3: Oh my! We'll wear them.

All Kittens: Thank you!
Now we'd like to share
something special with you.

All: Come on!
Let's all eat pie!

The End

4

Kitten 1: We're three little kittens.

Kitten 2: We've lost our mittens.

Kitten 3: Now we shall have no pie.

All Kittens: Oh my!

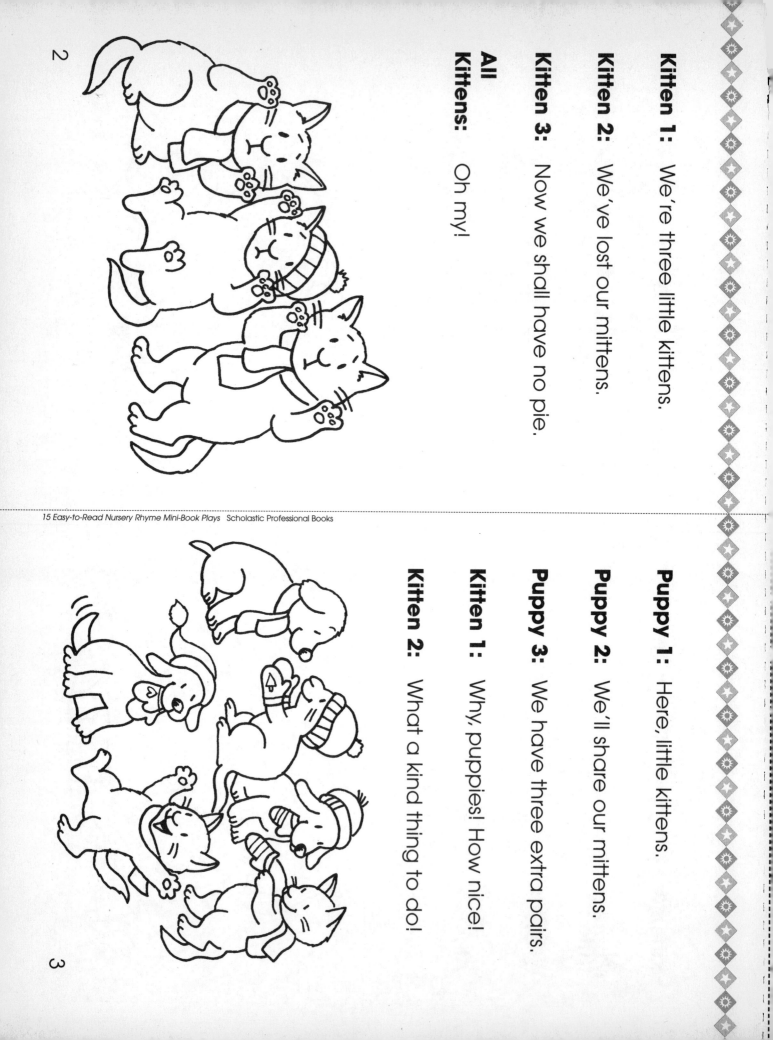

2

Puppy 1: Here, little kittens.

Puppy 2: We'll share our mittens.

Puppy 3: We have three extra pairs.

Kitten 1: Why, puppies! How nice!

Kitten 2: What a kind thing to do!

3

Wee Willie Winkie's Mixed-up Day

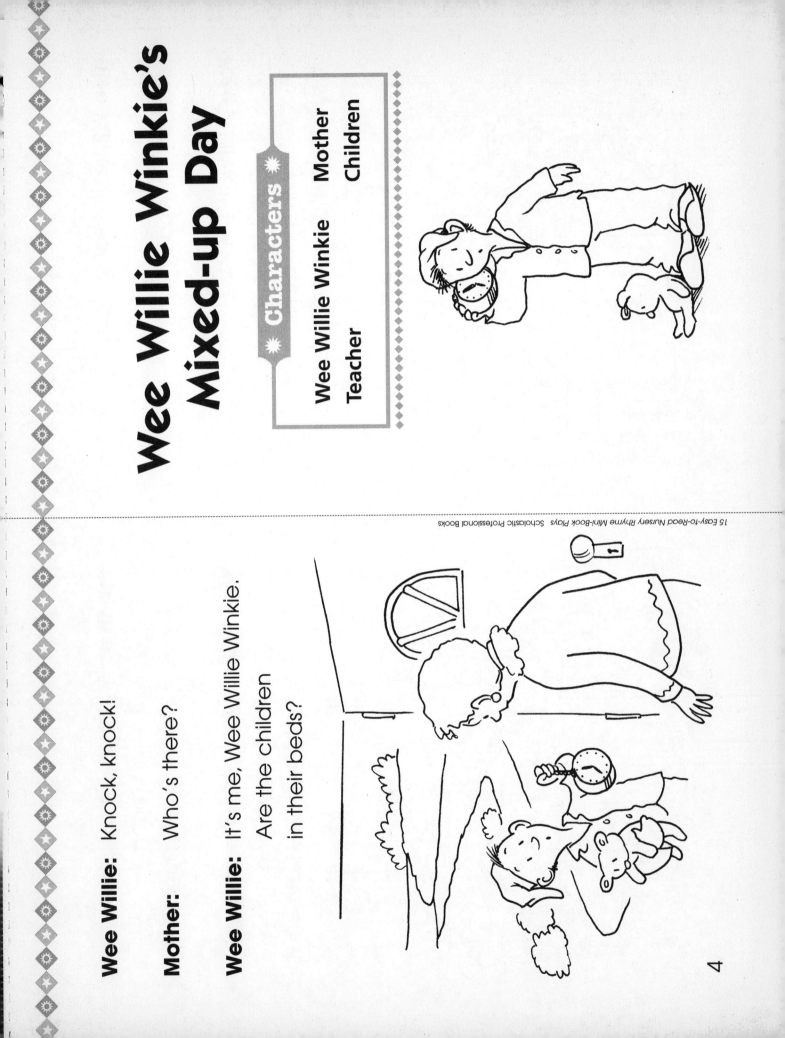

Characters

Wee Willie Winkie   Mother

Teacher   Children

Wee Willie: Knock, knock!

Mother: Who's there?

Wee Willie: It's me, Wee Willie Winkie.
Are the children
in their beds?

4

Wee Willie: Knock, knock!

Teacher: Who's there?

Wee Willie: It's me, Wee Willie Winkie.
Are the children
in their beds?

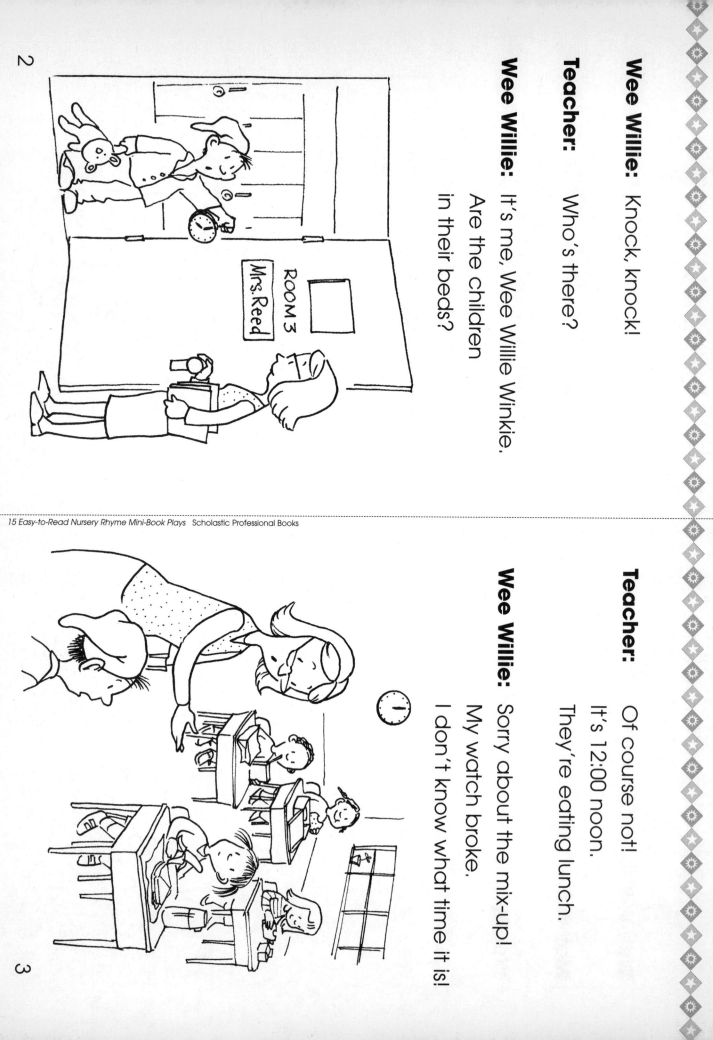

ROOM 3
Mrs. Reed

2

Teacher: Of course not!
It's 12:00 noon.
They're eating lunch.

Wee Willie: Sorry about the mix-up!
My watch broke.
I don't know what time it is!

3

Wee Willie: Knock, knock!

Mother: Who's there?

Wee Willie: It's me, Wee Willie Winkie.
Are the children
in their beds?
Now it's 8:00!

Children: Knock, knock!

Wee Willie: Who's there?

Children: It's us, the children.
We have a surprise!

Wee Willie: A new watch! Thanks!

TICK TOCK...

Children: Of course we are!

Zz-zz-zz-zz!

All: Good night!

The End

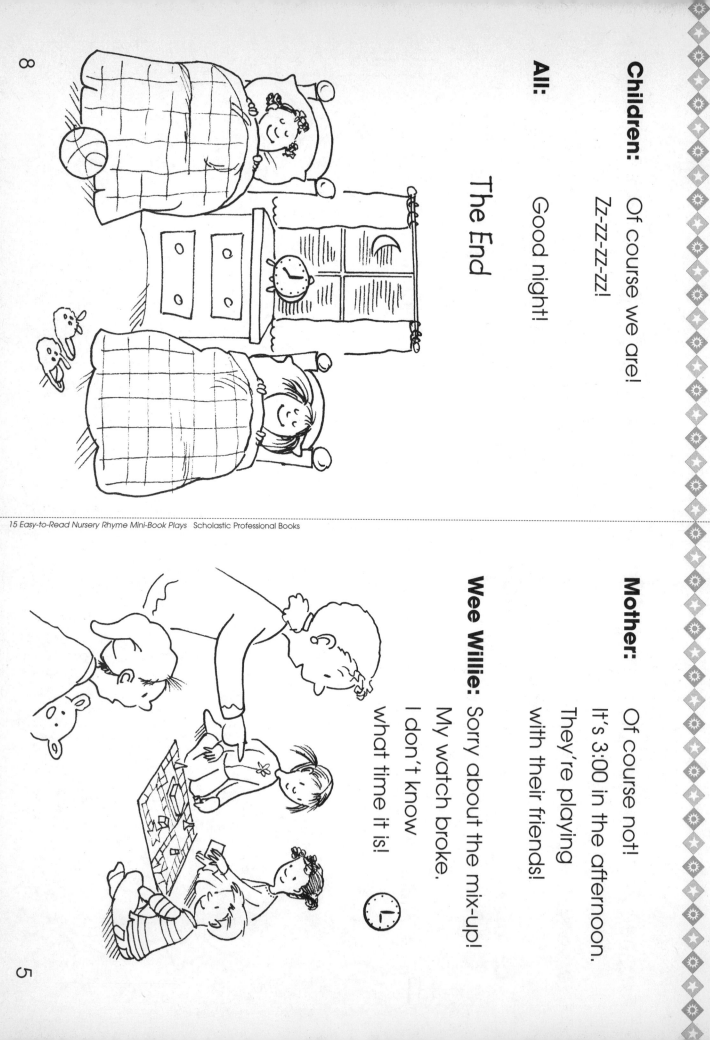

8

Mother: Of course not!

It's 3:00 in the afternoon.

They're playing

with their friends!

Wee Willie: Sorry about the mix-up!

My watch broke.

I don't know

what time it is!

5